Strangely familiar

In the Miocene and Pliocene ages, from about 20m to 2m years ago, many animals bore a strong resemblance to their modern descendants.

PROCOPTODON

pro-kop-toh-don "first cutting tooth"
10 ft (3 m) • 1.6m-10,000 years ago
This giant kangaroo moved fast
in huge leaps across the
Australian plains.

PALEOPARADOXIA

pal-ee-oh-para-dox-ee-ah "ancient marvel"
68 in (1.7 m)/600 lb (270 kg) • 20-10mya
Hippo-like Paleoparadoxia foraged through
the warm sea shallows for seaweed and clams.

MEGATHERIUM

meg-ah-thee-ree-um "great beast"
20 ft (6 m) • 3-1.6mya
This immense ground sloth could graze on the
treetops when it stood on its hind legs.

PHASCOLONUS

fass-col-oh-nus "moundlike"
hippo-sized • 5-3mya
Phascolonus was a giant
Australian wombat, a
pouched plant eater that lived
in herds.

TETRALOPHODON

tet-rah-loff-oh-don "four crest tooth"
10 ft (3 m) at shoulder • 10-3mya
Tetralophodon was a mastodon, a relative of
the elephant, and some males had 6 ft (2 m)
tusks curving down from their lower jaw.

TOXODON

tox-oh-don "bow tooth"
9 ft (2.7 m) • 5-2mya
Rhino-like Toxodon had a body like a barrel,
and consumed huge quantities of tough grass.

Tusks, horns, and fangs

In swamps and wetlands relatives of elephants rooted and scooped plants with specialized tusks, while other animals developed tough teeth for grazing, or fangs for stabbing their prey.

NESODON

nees-oh-don "island tooth"
5-6 ft (1.5-1.8 m) • 20-5mya
The teeth of rhino-like Nesodon kept growing as it wore them out eating the tough Pampas grasses of South America.

ANANCUS ARVERNENSIS

an-ank-us arv-er-nen-sis "with straight tusks, from the Auvergne"
10 ft (3 m) tall • 6-1mya
Swamp-dwelling Anancus, a member of the mastodon family related to elephants, had short legs, but its tusks were up to 13 ft (4 m) long.

TELEOCEROS

tel-ee-oss-er-us "perfect horn"
13 ft (4 m) • 15-5mya
This early rhino had a small nose horn, and its short-legged body was long and massive, and almost dragged on the ground.

PLATYBELODON

plat-ee-bel-oh-don "flat dart tooth"
10 ft (3 m) high • 10-5mya
Platybelodon was a shovel-tusker, which scooped up water plants with its flat-edged lower tusks.

SYNTHETICOCERAS

sin-thet-oss-er-as "compound skull"
6.6 ft (2 m) • 6-4mya
Syntheroceras was a small deerlike animal with a Y-shaped horn on its nose, which grazed the scrublands of North America in herds.

THYLACOSMILUS

thigh-lak-oh-smy-lus "pouched chisel"
4 ft (1.2 m) • 6-4mya
This saber-toothed cat, which had a pouch for its newborn young, stabbed its prey with its long fangs.

Packs and herds

Some plant eaters moved in herds, finding safety in numbers, but some meat eaters also traveled and hunted in packs.

EPIGAULUS

ep-ee-gaw-lus "upon bucket"
12 in (30 cm) • 23-5mya
This gopher-like burrowing rodent had an unusual pair of horns on its muzzle which it may have used to help dig its burrow.

GIRAFFOKERYX

jir-aff-oh-keh-rix "giraffe horn"
5 ft (1.5 m) at shoulder • 23-5mya
Giraffokerx had long forelegs, a sloping back, and two sets of knobbly horns.

HYPOHIPPUS

hy-poh-hip-us "low horse"
4 ft (1.2 m) tall • 17-11mya
Hypohippus had three-toed feet to carry it on soft forest floors, and had a long body but short legs.

BLASTOMERYX

blast-oh-meh-rix "growing ruminant"
30 in (75 cm)• 20-2mya
This small hornless deer browsed in the forest and dug for roots with its short tusks.

HEMICYON

hem-ee-ky-on "half dog"
5 ft (1.5 m) • 25-10mya
Hemicyon was a bear-dog which hunted in packs on the open plains of Asia, Europe, and North America.

DIMYLUS

dy-my-lus 'two grinders'
8 in (20 cm) • 23-5mya
Dimylus was an early relative of the hedgehog, and had a long snout, a long tail, and ate insects and worms.

South American families

Many creatures, including huge meat-eating flightless birds, evolved to take advantage of South American environments, but the ancestors of apes and humans evolved in Africa and Asia.

HOMALODOTHERIUM
hom-ah-low-doh-thee-ree-um "level beast"
6.6 ft (2 m) • 23-15mya
This large South American plant eater had clawed feet and stood on its hind legs to browse on low branches.

ALLODESMUS
al-oh-dez-mus "other chain"
6.6 ft (2 m) • 23-15mya
This early relative of sealions swam with broad flippers and could hear underwater.

PHORORACOS
for-oh-rak-os "bearing wrinkles"
Up to 6.6 ft (2 m) tall • up to 26-12mya
This tall, wingless, South American bird killed and devoured animals up to the size of sheep with its huge and powerful beak.

PROTYPOTHERIUM
pro-ty-poh-thee-ree-um "before the Typotheres"
20 in (51 cm) • 23-15mya
This rabbit-sized plant eater with long legs and a long tail scampered across the Argentine plains feeding on leaves.

NECROLESTES
nek-roh-less-tees "grave robber"
6 in (15 cm) • 23-15mya
Necrolestes was a molelike burrower with fine teeth for catching insects and worms.

PROTHYLACINUS
pro-thy-la-ky-nus "before pouched"
4 ft (1.2 m) • 23-15mya
This South American marsupial meat eater had short legs, and a doglike skull with big flesh-tearing teeth.

DRYOPITHECUS
dry-oh-pith-uh-kus "tree ape"
24 in (60 cm) • 25-10mya
Dryopithecus, from Africa and Asia, a fruit-eating ancestor of modern apes, had chimpanzee-like limbs, and climbed trees.

Grazers and browsers

A huge variety of plant eaters evolved to feed on the forests and grasslands covering the planet.

PLATYPITTAMYS

plat-ee-pit-ah-mis "flat burrow mouse"
12 in (30 cm) • 35-23mya
Platypittamys was a ratlike rodent from Patagonia, which used its front teeth to help dig its burrows.

INDRICOTHERIUM

in-drik-oh-theer-ee-um "Indrik (mythical animal) beast"
18 ft (5.4 m) at the shoulder/16.5 tons • 30mya
Indricotherium was the largest land mammal that ever lived, and browsed on the tops of trees.

ENTELODON

en-tel-oh-don "perfect teeth"
10 ft (3 m) long/3 ft (90 cm) at the shoulder
• 35-23mya
Entelodon looked like a warthog, with two pairs of bony knobs protruding sideways from its lower jaw.

CLADOSICTIS

klad-oh-sik-tis "early weasel"
32 in (80 cm) • 25-20my
Cladosictis was a marsupial; a mammal with a pouch for its young. It was similar to an otter, and hunted small mammals and reptiles.

CAINOTHERIUM

kane-oh-theer-ee-um "new beast"
12 in (30 cm) • 25-20mya
Cainotherium looked and behaved like a rabbit, with big ears, long hind legs and a bounding run, but also had hooves.

MERYCOIDODON

mer-ee-koid-oh-don "ruminant-form tooth"
56 in (1.4 m) • 33-20mya
Slow-moving Merycoidodon was a herd animal with a piglike head and chisel teeth which wandered the North American plains.

Familiar shapes

Early horselike animals were small compared to modern horses, but other species, such as relatives of the rhinoceros, were much larger than their modern descendants.

DINICTIS

dy-nik-tis "terrible weasel"
7 ft (2.2 m) including tail/110 lb (50 kg) • 30-20mya
The size of a puma, Dinictis was an ancestor of the cats, agile and cunning, with daggerlike stabbing teeth.

ARSINOITHERIUM

ar-sin-oy-thee-ree-um "Arsinoa's beast"
11 ft (3.4 m) long/6 ft (1.8 m) at the shoulder
• 35-30mya
Arsinoitherium lived in the swamps of Egypt, and was similar to a rhino, but had two horns side by side on its muzzle.

PYROTHERIUM

pie-roh-thee-ree-um "fire beast"
10 ft (3 m) long • 35-30mya
Pyrotherium looked like an elephant and had short legs, a massive body, a short trunk, and short tusks in both jaws.

HESPEROCYON

hesp-er-oh-ky-on "western dog'"
32 in (80 cm) • 30-20mya
Hesperocyon looked like a mongoose, but was an early relative of the dog.

RHYNCIPPUS

rin-kip-us "snout horse"
40 in (1 m) • 35-30mya
Rhyncippus, from South America, had a horselike head and grazing teeth, but had feet with claws.

BRONTOTHERIUM

bron-toh-thee-ree-um "thunder beast"
8 ft (2.5 m) high at the shoulder
• 35-30mya
Brontotherium was a gigantic rhino-like mammal which carried a large Y-shaped horn on its nose.

Strange ancestors

Some of the early relatives of modern animals looked very different from their descendants.

DAPHOENUS

da-fee-nus "blood colored"
5 ft (1.5 m) • 35-30mya
With its long tail, short limbs and spreading toes, Daphoenus was a bear-dog, an early relative of dogs and wolves.

ANDREWSARCHUS

and-roos-ar-kus "Andrews' ancient beast"
Up to 20 ft (6 m) long • 40-35mya
This huge hunter was the largest land-based meat-eating mammal that has ever lived, and had a skull 3 ft (1 m).

BASILOSAURUS

baz-il-oh-saw-rus "king lizard"
80 ft (25 m) • 40-35mya
Basilosaurus was not a lizard at all, but an early whale with a long, serpent-like body and pointed teeth for catching fish.

PALAELODUS

pal-ee-loh-dus "ancient"
24 in (60 cm) tall • 35-20mya
Palaelodus was a long-legged shorebird that may have hunted its food by swimming and diving like a duck.

MOERITHERIUM

mer-ee-thee-ree-um "part beast"
24 in (60 cm) high/440 lb (200 kg)
• 37-30mya
This swamp-dweller looked like a hippo, and was an ancestor of the animals with trunks.

OXAENA

ox-eye-een-uh "sharp hyaena"
34 in (85 cm) • 40-35mya
This catlike mammal, with a long body and short limbs, walked flat footed on its five-toed feet.

The mammals take over

Without the competition of dinosaurs, the plant-eating mammals grew large first, followed by the meat eaters that preyed on them.

PALAEOTHERIUM

pal-ee-oh-thee-ree-um "ancient beast"
30 in (75 cm) • 37-33mya
This descendant of early horses had three-toed feet, with a hoof on each toe.

KOPIDODON

kop-ee-doh-don "cleaver tooth"
24-30 in (60-75 cm) • 50mya
Kopidodon was an otterlike hunter with a long tail, and teeth suitable for crushing shellfish and killing fish.

PATRIOFELIS

pat-ree-oh-feel-is "cat ancestor"
5 ft (1.5 m) • 50-40mya
Patriofelis was the size of a bear, and had a catlike head, with powerful crushing jaws.

UINTATHERIUM

yoo-int-ah-thee-ree-um "Uinta beast"
11 ft (3.5 m) • 56-35mya
Uintatherium was the first really big mammal, and looked like a rhino, but had large tusks in its upper jaw and three sets of blunt horns on its head.

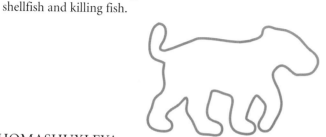

THOMASHUXLEYA

tom-as-hux-lee-ah named for the naturalist Thomas Huxley
4.3 ft (1.3 m) • 56-50mya
This sheep-sized mammal rooted around like a warthog with its tusks.

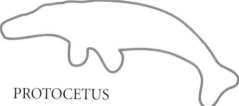

PROTOCETUS

pro-toh-see-tus "first whale"
8 ft (2.5 m) • 50-40mya
Protocetus lived in shallow coastal waters, catching fish in its narrow, tooth-lined jaws.

World without dinosaurs

The disappearance of the dinosaurs allowed mammals to evolve
to fill their place, but early mammal predators were small,
and the first big meat eaters in some regions were birds.

HYRACOTHERIUM

hy-rak-oh-thee-ree-um "Hyrax beast"
24 in (60 cm) • 58-50mya
The earliest known ancestor of the horse,
Hyracotherium was only 8 in (20 cm) high
at the shoulder.

PAKICETUS

pak-ee-see-tus "Pakistan whale"
6 ft (1.8 m) • 55-50mya
Pakicetus, the earliest known
whale, had paddle-like limbs and
spent much of its time on land.

CORYPHODON

kor-if-oh-don "top tooth"
7.4 ft (2.25 m) • 60-45mya
Coryphodon had a bulky body and hippo-like
tusks used to uproot swamp plants.

PARAMYS

par-ah-miss "beside mouse"
24 in (60 cm) • 60-45mya
This small squirrel-like
mammal is the first known
rodent, with constantly
growing gnawing teeth.

HYRACHYUS

hy-rah-ky-us "hyrax pig"
5 ft (1.5 m) • 55-35mya
A forerunner of the rhino, Hyrachyus could grip
and pluck vegetation with its upper lip.

DIATRYMA

die-ah-try-ma "two apertures"
6.6 ft (2 m) tall • 55-50mya
Diatryma was a huge flightless bird
with powerful legs and claws, and a
massive beak used to kill its prey.

The end of the dinosaurs

The great extinction of the dinosaurs around 65 million years ago may have been caused by a massive meteorite landing in eastern Mexico, and prepared the way for the Age of the Mammals.

HYOPSODUS

hy-op-sode-us "hog tooth"
20 in (50 cm) • 50-53mya
This short limbed plant-eating mammal kept its body close to the ground.

TYRANNOSAURUS

ty-ran-oh-saw-rus "tyrant lizard"
up to 50 ft (15 m) • 70-65mya
Tyrannosaurus was the ultimate killer dinosaur of North America, and heavier than an African elephant.

HADROSAURUS

had-roh-saw-rus "big lizard"
33 ft (10 m) • 80-65mya
Hadrosaurus, a typical duckbill, with a horny bill and hundreds of teeth at the back of the jaws, was the first dinosaur ever discovered in North America.

PHENACODUS

fen-ak-oh-dus "imposter tooth"
sheep-size • 58-50mya
Phenacodus was one of the earliest known plant-eating mammals with hooves on all its toes and fingers.

SINOPA

sine-ope-ah "red earth"
fox size • 60-50mya
Sinopa was a foxlike mammal, with sharp cheek teeth used to slice up flesh.

ORODROMEUS

or-oh-drom-ee-us "mountain runner"
8 ft (2.5 m) • 80-65mya
Orodromeus had a long stiff tail, which helped it balance when running and dodging.

THESCELOSAURUS

thes-kel-oh-saw-rus "wonderful lizard"
10-13 ft (3-4 m) • 80-65mya
These small plant eaters had hearts similar to birds, and may have been warm-blooded.

Drifting continents

Herds of duck-billed dinosaurs wandered across China and Mongolia as well as North America, but the main continents were now moving apart.

EUOPLOCEPHALUS

yoo-oh-ploh-sef-uh-lus "well armored head"
23 ft (7 m) • 80-65mya
Solitary Euoplocephalus, without the protection of a herd, carried a heavy two-headed club at the end of its long tail.

SHANTUNGASAURUS

shan-tung-ah-saw-rus "Shantung lizard"
Up to 50 ft (15m)/5 tons • 80-65mya
One of the largest of the duck-billed dinosaurs, Shantungasaurus, from China, had a massive, flat head and a tail taking up half its body length.

SAUROLOPHUS

saw-roh-loh-fus "ridged lizard"
up to 43 ft (13 m) • 80-65mya
Saurolophus, found in Mongolia and North America, may have been able to blow up skin flaps on its face like balloons to impress other herd members.

TARBOSAURUS

tar-boh-saw-rus "alarming lizard"
46 ft (14 m) • 80-65mya
Gigantic Tarbosaurus was one of the fiercest Mongolian flesh eaters, with its huge head, jaws and fangs.

PACHYCEPHALOSAURUS

pak-ee-kef-ah-loh-saw-rus "thick head lizard"
27 ft (8 m) • 80-65mya
The domed skull of this dinosaur was 8 in (20 cm) thick and used in butting contests.

GRYPOSAURUS

grip-oh-saw-rus "griffin lizard"
33 ft (10 m) • 80-65mya
This duck-billed dinosaur, like others of the same family, had no front teeth, but its jaw teeth were constantly replaced as they wore out.

PROSAUROLOPHUS

proh-saw-roh-loh-fus "before saurolophus"
27 ft (8 m) • 80-65mya
Herds of Prosaurolophus wandered across Canada, grazing on the ground and rearing up on hind legs to eat tree foliage.

Duck-billed trumpeters

The duck-billed dinosaurs were herd animals, and often had hollow crests on their heads which helped them make loud calls to other herd members.

CORYTHOSAURUS

koh-rith-oh-saw-rus "helmet crested lizard"
33 ft (10 m) • 80-65mya
This duck-billed dinosaur had a long bony crest, and grazed beside an ancient inland sea in western North America.

MAIASAURA

my-uh-saw-rah "good mother lizard"
30 ft (9 m) • 80-65mya
Maiasaura looked after its eggs and young in large nesting colonies.

TROODON

troo-oh-don "wounding tooth"
10 ft (3 m) • 80-65mya
Large-brained Troodon had the big eyes of a night hunter.

BRACHYLOPHOSAURUS

brak-ee-loh-foh-saw-rus "short crested lizard"
23 ft (7 m) • 80-65mya
Duck-billed dinosaurs like Brachylophosaurus had cutting teeth in their cheeks which were self-sharpening as they rubbed together.

DROMAEOSAURUS

droh-mee-oh-saw-rus "running lizard"
6 ft (1.8 m) • 80-65mya
This fast-running killer had long-fanged jaws and a deadly "sickle" claw on each foot.

OVIRAPTOR MONGOLIENSIS

ov-ee-rap-tor mon-goal-ee-en-sis "Mongolian egg thief"
6 ft (1.8 m) • 80-65mya
The scientists who found the first Oviraptor fossils thought it had stolen the fossil eggs found with it, but they turned out to be its own eggs.

PARASAUROLOPHUS

par-uh-saw-roh-loh-fus "side ridged lizard"
33 ft (10 m) • 80-65mya
Parasaurolophus was a large duckbilled plant eater and had a long curved crest on its head.

Swamps and plains

The large grazers were slow over the ground, but some birdlike dinosaurs moved fast on long legs.

HOMALOCEPHALE
hom-al-oh-kef-a-lee "even head"
10 ft (3 m) • 80-65mya
Homalocephale had a thick knobby skull used by males in pushing contests.

EDMONTOSAURUS
ed-mont-oh-saw-rus "Edmonton lizard"
Up to 43 ft (13 m)/3.8 tons • 80-65mya
A typical duck-billed dinosaur, Edmontosaurus cropped plants with its toothless beak and chewed them up with its close-packed cheek teeth.

SALTASAURUS
sal-tuh-saw-rus "Salta lizard"
39 ft (12 m) • 80-65mya
Saltasaurus was protected by a skin covered in bony studs and a whiplash tail.

AVIMIMUS
av-ee-my-mus "bird mimic"
5 ft (1.5 m) • 80-65mya
Avimimus was very birdlike, with a toothless beak, long hindlegs, and, possibly, feathered arms.

GALLIMIMUS
gal-ee-my-mus "chicken mimic"
Up to 20 ft (6 m) • 80-65mya
This large ostrich dinosaur had clawed hands for catching small creatures.

CENTROSAURUS
sent-roh-saw-rus "sharp point lizard"
20 ft (6 m) • 80-65mya
Powerful centrosaurus, a common horn-faced dinosaur, wandered North America in huge herds of several thousand individuals.

Killers large and small

The meat-eating dinosaurs were as varied as the plant eaters, and ranged from small, fast hunters to huge killing machines.

PROTOCERATOPS

proh-toh-sair-uh-tops "first horned face"
10 ft (3 m) • 80-65mya
Protoceratops wandered the Mongolian lowlands in herds grazing on low-growing shrubs and grasses.

DEINOCHEIRUS

die-noh-ky-rus "terrible hand"
Up to 6 tons • 80-65mya
Only the extraordinary arms of this dinosaur have been found, each 8 ft (2.4 m) long, with three long, curved claws.

STYGIMOLOCH

sty-gee-moh-lok "River of Hell devil"
20 ft (6 m) • 80-65mya
Stygimoloch probably used its domed skull, bristling with bony horns and spikes, in butting contests.

LAMBEOSAURUS

lam-bee-oh-saw-rus "Lambe's lizard"
Up to 50 ft (15 m) • 80-65mya
This large duck-billed dinosaur had a hollow crest which helped it to make loud calls to others.

CHIROSTENOTES

ky-roh-sten-oh-teez "slender hands"
6.6 ft (2 m) • 80-65mya
Small and light, Chirostenotes was probably a hunter, and had long, narrow fingers with long claws.

ALBERTOSAURUS

al-bert-oh-sau-rus "Alberta lizard"
27 ft (8 m)/up to 2 tons • 80-65mya
Meat-eating Albertosaurus ran on two legs, and seized its prey in enormous jaws lined with backward-pointing teeth.

PACHYRHINOSAURUS

pak-ee-ry-noh-saw-rus "thick nosed lizard"
18 ft (5.5 m) • 80-65mya
Sturdy pachyrhinosaurus had a bony growth along the top of its muzzle.

Predators beware

By the Late Cretaceous period there was a huge variety of dinosaurs, but all would die out by its end, about 65 million years ago.

TRICERATOPS

try-sair-uh-tops "three horned face"
30 ft (9 m) • 80-65mya
Massive Triceratops was the largest of the "horn-faced" dinosaurs, and, like a rhino, charged any threat.

EDMONTONIA

ed-mon-toe-nee-uh "from Edmonton"
23 ft (7 m) • 80-64mya
Edmontonia's armor included large shoulder spikes, and bony shields and plates. It was very low-slung to protect its soft belly.

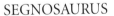

SEGNOSAURUS

seg-noh-saw-rus "slow lizard"
30 ft (9 m) • 80-65mya
Segnosaurus probably used its small, sharp cheek teeth for holding and chewing fish.

CHASMOSAURUS

kaz-moh-saw-rus "chasm lizard"
16 ft (5 m) • 80-65mya
The huge bony neck frill and long face horns of Chasmosaurus scared off attackers and attracted mates.

PINACOSAURUS

pin-ak-oh-saw-rus "plank lizard"
18 ft (5.5 m) • 80-65mya
A blow from the bony club at the end of Pinacosaurus's powerful tail could be lethal to an unwary meat eater.

DROMICEIOMIMUS

drom-ee-say-oh-my-mus "emu mimic"
11 ft (3.5 m)/220 lb (100 kg) • 80-65mya
This dinosaur had keen eyes for night hunting, and may have been warm-blooded to deal with freezing conditions.

The battle for survival

The flesh eaters depended on their speed, fangs, and claws, while their prey found safety in horns and thick armor.

STYRACOSAURUS

styr-ra-koh-saw-rus "spiked lizard"
18 ft (5.5 m) • 80-65mya
Its massive horned head, with its spiky frill, made Styracosaurus a difficult target for would-be predators.

GARUDIMIMUS

ga-roo-di-my-mus "Garuda (mythical bird) mimic"
11 ft (3.5 m) • 100-75mya
Garudimimus used its long, stiff tail for balance as it moved fast across the flatlands of Mongolia.

SPINOSAURUS

spy-noh-saw-rus "thorn lizard'"
33 ft (10 m)/4 tons • 80-65mya
This large African hunter had spines over 5 ft (1.5 m) long supporting the sail along its back.

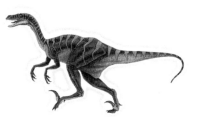

VELOCIRAPTOR

vel-oss-ee-rap-tor "quick plunderer"
6 ft (1.8 m) • 80-65mya
This large-brained, ferocious hunter probably worked in packs.

STRUTHIOMIMUS

strooth-ee-oh-my-mus "ostrich mimic"
13 ft (4 m) • 80-65mya
This "ostrich" dinosaur had long arms with three-clawed hands, and could run at up to 50 mph (80km/h).

HESPERORNIS

hess-per-awr-nis "western bird"
5 ft (1.5 m) • 80-65mya
This diving bird was clumsy on land, and had teeth in its long, pointed beak.

Stickers for fun

Here are some stickers just for fun. Check with an adult before you stick them to anything.

Avimimus

Pteranodon

Kentrosaurus

Allosaurus

Archaeopteryx

Dicraeosaurus

Strangely familiar

In the Miocene and Pliocene ages, from about 20m to 2m years ago, many animals bore a strong resemblance to their modern descendants.

Tetralophodon

Toxodon

Procoptodon

Paleoparadoxia

Megatherium

Phascolonus

Tusks, horns, and fangs

In swamps and wetlands relatives of elephants rooted and scooped plants with specialized tusks, while other animals developed tough teeth for grazing, or fangs for stabbing their prey.

Thylacosmilus

Platybelodon

Anancus arvernensis

Syntheticoceras

Teleoceros

Nesodon

Packs and herds

Some plant eaters moved in herds, finding safety in numbers, but some meat eaters also traveled and hunted in packs.

Hypohippus

Dimylus

Epigaulus

Hemicyon

Blastomeryx

Giraffokeryx

South American families

Many creatures, including huge meat-eating flightless birds, evolved to take advantage of South American environments, but the ancestors of apes and humans evolved in Africa and Asia.

Prothylacinus

Allodesmus

Homalodotherium

Dryopithecus

Phororacos

Necrolestes

Protypotherium

Grazers and browsers

A huge variety of plant eaters evolved to feed on the forests and grasslands covering the planet.

Indricotherium

Cladosictis

Platypittamys

Entelodon

Cainotherium

Merycoidodon

Familiar shapes

Early horselike animals were small compared to modern horses, but other species, such as relatives of the rhinoceros, were much larger than their modern descendants.

Brontotherium

Pyrotherium

Hesperocyon

Dinictis

Arsinoitherium

Rhyncippus

Strange ancestors

Some of the early relatives of modern animals looked very different from their descendants.

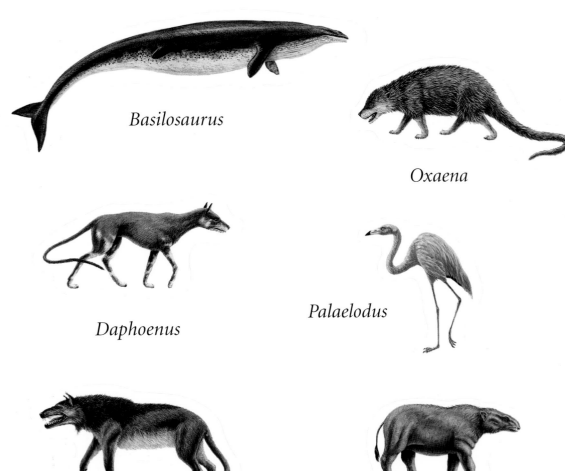

Basilosaurus

Oxaena

Daphoenus

Palaelodus

Andrewsarchus

Moeritherium

The mammals take over

Without the competition of dinosaurs, the plant-eating mammals grew large first, followed by the meat eaters that preyed on them.

Thomashuxleya

Protocetus

Uintatherium

Palaeotherium

Kopidodon

Patriofelis

World without dinosaurs

The disappearance of the dinosaurs allowed mammals to evolve to fill their place, but early mammal predators were small, and the first big meat eaters in some regions were birds.

Diatryma

Coryphodon

Pakicetus

Hyracotherium

Hyrachyus

Paramys

The end of the dinosaurs

The great extinction of the dinosaurs around 65 million years ago may have been caused by a massive meteorite landing in eastern Mexico, and prepared the way for the age of the mammals.

Phenacodus

Sinopa

Hadrosaurus

Thescelosaurus

Orodromeus

Tyrannosaurus

Hyopsodus

Drifting continents

Herds of duck-billed dinosaurs wandered across China and Mongolia as well as North America, but the main continents were now moving apart.

Pachycephalosaurus

Shantungasaurus

Prosaurolophus

Tarbosaurus

Gryposaurus

Euoplocephalus

Saurolophus

Duck-billed trumpeters

The duck-billed dinosaurs were herd animals, and often had hollow crests on their heads which helped them make loud calls to other herd members.

Brachylophosaurus

Troodon

Dromaeosaurus

Oviraptor mongoliensis

Maiasaura

Parasaurolophus

Corythosaurus

Swamps and plains

The large grazers were slow over the ground, but some
birdlike dinosaurs moved fast on long legs.

Centrosaurus

Gallimimus

Avimimus

Edmontosaurus

Saltasaurus

Homalocephale

Killers large and small

The meat-eating dinosaurs were as varied as the plant eaters, and ranged from small, fast hunters to huge killing machines.

Deinocheirus

Lambeosaurus

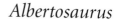
Albertosaurus

Chirostenotes

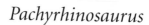
Pachyrhinosaurus

Stygimoloch

Protoceratops

Predators beware

By the Late Cretaceous period there was a huge variety of dinosaurs, but all would die out by its end about 65 million years ago.

Pinacosaurus

Edmontonia

Dromiceiomimus

Triceratops

Segnosaurus

Chasmosaurus

The battle for survival

The flesh eaters depended on their speed, fangs, and claws, while their prey found safety in horns and thick armor.

Garudimimus

Spinosaurus

Hesperornis

Struthiomimus

Styracosaurus

Velociraptor

Weird and wonderful

There was a huge variety of dinosaur shapes, from long-legged plains dwellers to tanklike grazers.

Archaeornithomimus

Muttaburrasaurus

Minmi

Wuerhosaurus

Ouranosaurus

Pteranodon

Speed and armor

In the fight for survival some plant eaters developed heavy armor, while others became fast runners, or moved in herds.

Baryonyx

Acrocanthosaurus

Stegoceras

Sauropelta

Astrodon

Hypsilophodon

Giant appetites

Large plant eaters had to devour vast
quantities of vegetation to stay alive.

Carnotaurus

Iguanodon

Leaellynasaura

Camptosaurus

Psittacosaurus

Deinonychus

Brachiosaurus

Dominant Dinosaurs

Throughout the Age of Dinosaurs other animal forms
continued to evolve, although the dinosaurs were dominant.

Peloneustes

Ornitholestes

Camarasaurus

Compsognathus

Kentrosaurus

Rhamphoryncus

Towering giants

The gigantic sauropod dinosaurs developed extraordinarily long necks to enable them to reach the treetops, with some as tall as a five-story building.

Coelurus

Diplodocus

Apatosaurus

Ceratosaurus

Stegosaurus

Mamenchisaurus

Larger and larger

The bigger the plant eaters became, the bigger grew the meat eaters that fed on them.

Yangchuanosaurus

Allosaurus

Dicraeosaurus

Archaeopteryx

Barosaurus

Tuojiangosaurus

Survival of the fittest

Many creatures developed weapons of defense
against ferocious hunters.

Yandusaurus

Pterodactyl

Shunosaurus

Cetiosaurus

Aellopos

Dryosaurus

Air, sea, and land

Some reptiles could fly, and others lived in water,
but dinosaurs lived on land.

Megalosaurus

Plesiosaurus

Dimorphodon

Eustreptospondylus

Gasosaurus

Ichthyosaur

Increasing in size

Many families of dinosaurs grew larger as time passed.

Heterodontosaurus

Massospondylus

Anchisaurus

Scelidosaurus

Dilophosaurus

Lesothosaurus

Hunters and hunted

As the planet became warmer and wetter, some dinosaurs feasted on the rich plant life, and meat-eating dinosaurs hunted the plant eaters.

Eurhinosaurus

Thecodontosaurus

Mussaurus

Protosuchus

Oligokyphus

Lufengosaurus

The dinosaurs flourish

200 million years ago there were increasing numbers of both meat- and plant-eating dinosaurs, and also the first small mammals.

Syntarsus

Melanosaurus

Megazostradon

Plateosaurus

Coelophysis

Riojasaurus

The beginning of dinosaurs

The Triassic period stretched from 245 to 208 million years ago, and the first small dinosaurs appeared about halfway through it.

Proganochelys

Herrerasaurus

Staurikosaurus

Gerrothorax

Mastodonsaurus

Mixosaurus

The first great extinction

About 245 million years ago many animal families suddenly died out, perhaps due to a meteorite hitting Earth, and other creatures took their place.

Aphaneramma

Dicynodonts

Nothosaurus

Placodus

Thrinaxodon

Triadobatracus

The move to the land

The reptiles were the first backboned
animals to live entirely on dry land.

Sauroctonus

Moschops

Mesosaurus

Diplocaulus

Varanosaurus

Dimetrodon

The age of fishes

Some fishes developed into amphibians,
four-legged animals that laid their eggs in water.

Eogyrinus

Dolichosoma

Pleurocanthus

Branchiosaurus

Bothriolepis

Dunkleosteus

Weird and wonderful

There was a huge variety of dinosaur shapes, from long-legged plains dwellers to tanklike grazers.

OURANOSAURUS

oo-ran-oh-saw-rus "brave lizard"
23 ft (7 m) • 145-135mya
Ouranosaurus warmed up extra fast in the African sun with the aid of the long "sail" along its back.

PTERANODON

ter-an-oh-don "toothless flier"
23 ft (7 m) wingspan • 110-90mya
Huge-winged Pteranodon soared for great distances over the seas in its search for fish.

MINMI

min-my after Minmi Crossing, Australia
6.6 ft (2 m) • 145-135mya
Minmi grazed on all fours and had bony protective shields inside its skin.

ARCHAEORNITHOMIMUS

ark-ee-or-nith-oh-my-mus "ancient bird mimic"
10 ft (3 m) • 110-90mya
This early "ostrich" dinosaur moved fast over flat plains on its long legs.

WUERHOSAURUS

where-oh-saw-rus "Wuerho lizard"
20 ft (6 m) • 145-135mya
The short, square bony plates along the back of this dinosaur may have been to protect it as it grazed with its head low.

MUTTABURRASAURUS

mut-uh-buh-ruh-saw-rus "Muttaburra lizard"
33 ft (10 m) • 100-75mya
This Australian plant eater may have used the bump on its head to help produce bellowing calls.

Speed and armor

In the fight for survival some plant eaters developed heavy
armor, while others became fast runners, or moved in herds.

SAUROPELTA

saw-roh-pel-ta "lizard shield"
25 ft (7.6 m) • 145-135mya
Sauropelta had bands of bony shields
along its back for protection.

HYPSILOPHODON

hip-sil-off-oh-don "high ridge tooth"
7.6 ft (2.3 m) • 145-135mya
Cautious Hypsilophodon avoided the big meat eaters by
being small and fast, and able to store food in cheek pouches.

STEGOCERAS

steg-oh-ser-as "horny roof"
6.6 ft (2 m) • 70mya
Lightweight and long-legged,
Stegoceras was an agile fast-
mover, armored with
a thick, bony skull
for dueling
with rivals.

ACROCANTHOSAURUS

ak-roh-can-thuh-saw-rus "top spined lizard"
40 ft (12 m)/3 tons • 145-135mya
This large hunter had a tall backbone ridge,
probably to help control body heat.

ASTRODON

ass-troh-don "star tooth"
33 ft (10 m) • 145-135mya
Astrodon had teeth like spoon-
shaped chisels to deal
with tough plants.

BARYONYX

bar-ee-on-ix "heavy claw"
30 ft (9 m) long/10 ft (3 m) tall/2 tons • 145-135mya
Baryonyx was a heavyweight which caught fish in its
crocodile-like jaws.

Giant appetites

Large plant eaters had to devour vast quantities of vegetation to stay alive.

DEINONYCHUS

die-non-ee-kus "terrible claw"
11 ft (3.4 m) • 145-135mya
Deinonychus ran on its back legs, and on each foot was a special large, curved claw that swiveled into place when attacking a victim.

IGUANODON

ig-wahn-oh-don "iguana tooth"
33 ft (10 m)/5 tons • 146-120mya
Herds of Iguanodons wandered through humid wetlands all over the planet, grazing on ferns and other plants with their horny beaks.

LEAELLYNASAURA

Lay-ell-lye-nuh-saw-ruh "Leaellyn's lizard"
40 in (1 m) • 150mya
This small dinosaur had large eyes to see in the long, gloomy Antarctic winters.

PSITTACOSAURUS

sih-tak-oh-saw-rus "parrot lizard"
6.6 ft (2 m) • 145-135mya
Psittacosaurus used its parrotlike beak to cut through tough plants.

BRACHIOSAURUS

brak-ee-oh-saw-rus "arm lizard"
80 ft (25 m) long/54 ft (16 m) high/50 tons • 150-120mya
This giant had a tiny mouth, and needed to swallow huge amounts of vegetation every day, so must hardly ever have stopped eating.

CAMPTOSAURUS

kamp-toh-saw-rus "bent lizard"
23 ft (7 m) • 140-120mya
Camptosaurus's hind legs were much longer than its forelegs, but both toes and fingers ended in hooves, so it was able to walk on all fours.

CARNOTAURUS

kar-noh-taw-rus "meat-eating bull"
25 ft (7.5 m) • 145-135mya
Despite its slim legs and body, Carnotaurus had a huge, horned, bull-like head.

Dominant dinosaurs

Throughout the age of dinosaurs other animal forms
continued to evolve, although the dinosaurs were dominant.

CAMARASAURUS

kam-uh-ruh-saw-rus "chambered lizard"
60 ft (18 m) • 160-146mya
Camarasaurus wandered all over North
America, and although bulky, had very
light bones.

RHAMPHORYNCHUS

ram-foe-rink-us "prow beak"
40 in (1 m) wingspan • 160-146mya
Rhamphoryncus used its long tail to keep
it steady as it flew low over the waves
trapping fish in its jaws.

ORNITHOLESTES

orn-ith-oh-lest-ees "bird robber"
6.6 ft (2 m) • 160-145mya
Only one fossil of Ornitholestes has ever been
found, and it probably ate birds, frogs, lizards, and
even small mammals.

PELONEUSTES

pel-oh-noo-stees "swimming monster"
10 ft (3 m) • 160-146mya
Streamlined Peloneustes swam swiftly to
catch squid and fish in its long jaws.

COMPSOGNATHUS

komp-sog-nay-thus "delicate jaw"
6.6 ft (2 m) • 160-146mya
This small European dinosaur
snatched up small creatures such as
lizards in the claws of its long fingers.

KENTROSAURUS

kent-roh-saw-rus "spiky lizard"
16 ft (5 m) • 160-146mya
Flesh eaters would have had a difficult time
attacking Kentrosaurus with its bristling spikes
and jutting bony plates.

Towering giants

The gigantic sauropod dinosaurs developed extraordinarily long necks to enable them to reach the treetops, with some as tall as a five-story building.

CERATOSAURUS

seh-rat-oh-saw-rus "horned lizard"
20 ft (6 m) • 160-146mya
Like a rhino, Ceratosaurus had a nose horn, and also had horns over its eyes.

STEGOSAURUS

steg-oh-saw-rus "roofed lizard"
30 ft (9 m) • 160-146mya
Stegosaurus may have used the double row of upright plates along its back to help control its temperature.

DIPLODOCUS

Dip-lo-doh-kus "double beam"
90 ft (27 m) • 160-145mya
Diplodocus is famous as one of the largest of all the dinosaurs.

APATOSAURUS

uh-pat-oh-saw-rus "deceptive lizard"
63 ft (21 m) • 160-146mya
Apatosaurus needed legs like pillars to carry its weight, but only had a tiny brain.

MAMENCHISAURUS

mah-men-kee-saw-rus "Mamen Brook lizard"
82 ft (25 m) • 160-146mya
This Chinese sauropod had the longest neck of all time, at up to 50 ft (15 m).

COELURUS

see-loo-rus "hollow tail"
6 ft (1.8 m) • 160-146mya
Small speedy Coelurus fed on small creatures, but may have run in packs to deal with larger ones.

Larger and larger

The bigger the plant eaters became, the bigger grew the meat eaters that fed on them.

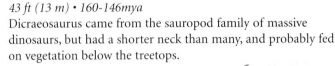

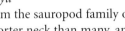

DICRAEOSAURUS
die-cree-uh-saw-rus "forked lizard"
43 ft (13 m) • 160-146mya
Dicraeosaurus came from the sauropod family of massive dinosaurs, but had a shorter neck than many, and probably fed on vegetation below the treetops.

YANGCHUANOSAURUS
yang-chwan-oh-saw-rus "Yangchuan lizard"
33 ft (10 m) • 160-146mya
This huge-jawed killer used its long tail for balance as it attacked its prey.

ARCHAEOPTERYX
ar-key-op-tuh-rix "ancient wing"
Up to 40 in (1 m) long • 160-146mya
Archaeopteryx had a bird's feathers and feet, but a reptile's teeth and bony tail.

TUOJIANGOSAURUS
toh-hwang-oh-saw-rus "Tuo River lizard"
23 ft (7 m) • 160-146mya
This armored dinosaur had a tiny brain and a dragon-like body with spikes and bony plates jutting from its back and tail.

BAROSAURUS
bar-oh-saw-rus "heavy lizard"
Up to 90 ft (27 m) long • 160-146mya
With a neck 30 ft (9 m) long, Barosaurus could easily feed on treetop vegetatation.

ALLOSAURUS
all-oh-saw-rus "different lizard"
40 ft (12 m) and up to 5 tons •
150-130mya
Allosaurus may have brought down the largest plant eaters by biting huge chunks out of the victim until it bled to death.

Survival of the fittest

Many creatures developed weapons of defense against ferocious hunters.

AELLOPOS
ee-loh-pos "storm footed"
5 ft (1.5 m) • 165-146mya
Related to the sharks, Aellopus had fins like wings and a spiked, whiplash tail.

PTERODACTYL
terr-oh-dak-til "wing finger"
30 in (75 cm) wingspan • 160-146mya
Pterodactyls swooped low over the sea to catch fish in their spike-toothed jaws.

DRYOSAURUS
dri-oh-saw-rus "oak lizard"
10-13 ft (3-4 m) • 175-150mya
Dryosaurus, like many other medium-sized plant eaters, used speed and agility as its main defense, and may have reached speeds up to 25 mph (40 km/h).

SHUNOSAURUS
shoo-nuh-saw-rus "Shuo lizard"
33 ft (10 m) • 175mya
Shunosaurus wielded a bony club and four sharp spikes at the end of its long tail.

CETIOSAURUS
seet-ee-oh-saw-rus "whale lizard"
70 ft (18.3 m) and over 10 tons in weight • 175-150mya
Cetiosaurus was one of the largest land animals that ever lived.

YANDUSAURUS
yan-doo-saw-rus "Yandu lizard"
5 ft (1.5 m) • 175mya
This fast-moving dinosaur dodged attackers with the aid of its long, stiff tail.

Air, sea, and land

Some reptiles could fly, and others lived in water, but dinosaurs lived on land.

DIMORPHODON

die-morf-oh-don "two types of teeth"
5 ft (1.5 m) wingspan • 208-190mya
This flying lizard had wings of skin, a long tail and a big beak lined with teeth.

EUSTREPTOSPONDYLUS

yew-strep-toh-spon-dee-lus "well curved vertebra"
23 ft (7 m) • 175mya
Eustreptospondylus ran on its hind legs and had saw-edged teeth.

MEGALOSAURUS

meg-uh-loh-saw-rus "great lizard"
30 ft (9 m) • 208-140mya
The first dinosaur ever named, Megalosaurus was a strong, heavy meat eater.

ICHTHYOSAUR

ik-thio-sawr "fish lizard"
6.6 ft (2 m) • 208-90mya
This dolphin-like reptile fed on fish and gave birth to live young at sea.

PLESIOSAURUS

pless-ee-oh-saw-rus "near lizard"
8 ft (2.5 m) • 208-190mya
With a streamlined body, long neck, and flippers, Plesiosaurus was an agile swimmer as it hunted fish and squid.

GASOSAURUS

gas-oh-saw-rus "gas reptile"
13 ft (4 m) • 175mya
Gasosaurus was a fast runner, and may have hunted in packs.

Increasing in size

Many families of dinosaurs grew larger as time passed.

LESOTHOSAURUS

luh-so-toh-saw-rus "Lesotho lizard"
40 in (1 m) • 208-190mya
This plant eater's hollow bones gave
it the lightness and speed
to avoid trouble.

HETERODONTOSAURUS

Het-uh-roh-dont-oh-saw-rus "different toothed lizard"
4 ft (1.2 m) • 208-190mya
Heterodontosaurus had some teeth for chopping, some for grinding,
and tusks for digging roots and scaring rivals.

DILOPHOSAURUS

die-loff-uh-saw-rus "two ridged lizard"
20 ft (6 m) • 208-190mya
Dilophosaurus weighed about half
a ton, and ran on its hind legs
after its prey.

ANCHISAURUS

an-kee-saw-rus "near lizard"
8 ft (2.4 m) • 208-190mya
About sheep-sized,
Anchisaurus was the
first dinosaur
discovered in the
United States.

SCELIDOSAURUS

skel-id-oh-saw-rus "limb lizard"
13 ft (4 m) • 208-190mya
Scelidosaurus protected its heavy,
low-slung body with rows of
bony studs.

MASSOSPONDYLUS

mass-oh-spon-die-lus "massive vertebra"
16 ft (5 m) • 208-190mya
Massospondylus swallowed stones to help
grind up to the tough vegetation it ate.

Hunters and hunted

As the planet became warmer and wetter, some dinosaurs feasted on the rich plant life, and meat-eating dinosaurs hunted the plant eaters.

MUSSAURUS

muh-saw-rus "mouse lizard"
10 ft (3 m) • 210-190mya
Mussaurus was named "mouse lizard" because the first ones discovered were young just out of their eggs, and only 8 in (20 cm) long.

OLIGOKYPHUS

ol-ig-oh-ky-fus "small curved animal"
20 in (50 cm) • 210-190mya
Although resembling a weasel-like mammal, Oligokyphus was a reptile.

THECODONTOSAURUS

theek-oh-dont-uh-saw-rus "socket toothed lizard"
7 ft (2 m) • 210-190mya
Thecodontosaurus was a plant eater equipped with huge thumb claws for protection against predators.

PROTOSUCHUS

pro-toh-soo-kus "first crocodile"
40 in (1 m) • 210-190mya
Protosuchus was an early crocodile but spent most of its time on land.

LUFENGOSAURUS

loo-feng-oh-saw-rus "Lufeng lizard"
20 ft (6 m) • 208-190mya
Lufengosaurus had a long neck, a bulky body, broad feet and huge thumb claws.

EURHINOSAURUS

yew-ryn-oh-saw-rus "good nose lizard"
6.6 ft (2 m) • 208-190mya
Seagoing Eurhinosaurus had a long upper jaw lined with teeth like a chainsaw.

The dinosaurs flourish

200 million years ago there were increasing numbers of both meat- and plant-eating dinosaurs, and also the first small mammals.

COELOPHYSIS
see-loh-fie-sis "hollow form"
10 ft (3 m) • 220-208mya
Coelophysis was light and fast, and hunted in packs.

RIOJASAURUS
ree-oh-juh-saw-rus "La Rioja lizard"
33 ft (10 m) • 220-208mya
With very short front legs, the dinosaur Riojasaurus could graze on the ground, or reach up with its long neck into the trees.

SYNTARSUS
sin-tar-sus "fused ankle"
10 ft (3 m) • 215-200mya
Running on its slender hind legs, Syntarsus hunted lizards and slow plant eaters.

PLATEOSAURUS
play-tee-oh-saw-rus "flat lizard"
27 ft (8 m) • 220-208mya
Plateosaurus probably used its long tail as a support when it reared up.

MEGAZOSTRADON
meg-ah-zoh-stra-don "big girdled tooth"
5 in (12 cm) • 205-190mya
Tiny Megazostradon was one of the first true mammals, and hunted insects at night.

MELANOSAURUS
mel-an-oh-saw-rus "black mountain lizard"
40 ft (12 m) • 220-208mya
One of the earliest plant-eating dinosaurs, Melanosaurus carried its great weight on elephant-like legs.

The beginning of dinosaurs

The Triassic period stretched from 245 to 208 million years ago, and the first small dinosaurs appeared about halfway through it.

GERROTHORAX

ger-oh-thaw-rax "shield trunk"
40 in (1 m) • 220-208mya
The amphibian Gerrothorax had a broad, armored body and head, external gills, and tiny limbs which were almost useless.

STAURIKOSAURUS

stor-ik-oh-saw-rus "(Southern) Cross lizard"
6.6 ft (2 m) • 230-220mya
Fast-running Staurikosaurus was one of the first meat-eating dinosaurs.

MIXOSAURUS

mix-oh-saur-us "mixed reptile"
40 in (1 m) • 225mya
Its fishlike body and paddle-like limbs made Mixosaurus an excellent swimmer.

MASTODONSAURUS

mast-oh-don-saw-rus "mastodon lizard"
16-20 ft (5-6 m) • 240-220mya
With a huge head like an alligator, Mastodonsaurus was one of the biggest amphibians that ever lived.

HERRERASAURUS

huh-rare-uh-saw-rus "Herrera's reptile"
10 ft (3 m) • 230mya
Herrerasaurus was an early dinosaur, and had curved claws to grasp its prey.

PROGANOCHELYS

pro-gah-noh-chel-is "first turtle"
24 in (61 cm) • 210mya
Unlike modern turtles, Proganochelys could not hide its head and limbs inside its shell, and had teeth as well as a beak.

The first great extinction

About 245 million years ago many animal families suddenly died out, perhaps due to a meteorite hitting Earth, and other creatures took their place.

PLACODUS

plak-oh-dus "flat tooth"
6.6 ft (2 m) • 230-220mya
Sluggish Placodus crushed shellfish with flat, grinding back teeth.

DICYNODONTS

dy-cy-noh-donts "two dog-like teeth"
From rat to hippo-size • 250-240mya
Members of the Dicynodont family cropped plants with their horny beaks and flourished all over the planet.

NOTHOSAURUS

noth-oh-saw-rus "false lizard"
10 ft (3 m) • 245-225mya
Streamlined swimmer Nothosaurus hunted fish and squid, but could clamber ashore to rest.

THRINAXODON

thrin-ax-oh-don "trident tooth"
20 in (50 cm) • 245-240mya
This solidly built little hunter may have had hair to help control its body heat.

APHANERAMMA

a-fan-er-ama "invisible girdle"
24 in (60 cm) • 245-240mya
Aphaneramma's head took up a third of its body length, and it lived on sea fish.

TRIADOBATRACUS

tri-ad-oh-bat-rah-kus "Triassic frog"
4 in (10 cm) • 245-240mya
Triadobatracus is the first known fossil frog, and had the remnants of a tail.

The move to the land

The reptiles were the first backboned
animals to live entirely on dry land.

DIPLOCAULUS

dy-ploh-caw-lus "twin stems"
40 in (1 m) • 280-275mya
The 'wings' on its head helped
Diplocaulus to swim, and to
avoid being eaten.

MOSCHOPS

mos-kops "cow-face"
Up to 16 ft (5 m) • 260-250my.
Vegetarian Moschops may have used its massive skull for butting rivals.

VARANOSAURUS

va-ran-oh-saw-rus "monitor lizard reptile"
5 ft (1.5 m) • 280-270mya
Varanosaurus had long jaws and spiky
teeth, ideal for catching fish.

SAUROCTONUS

Saw-rok-tone-us "lizard killer"
14 ft (4.2 m) • 250-245mya
Sauroctonus was a ferocious killer
with a heavy build and large teeth.

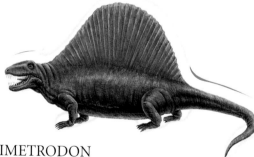

MESOSAURUS

mess-oh-saw-rus "middle reptile"
40 in (1 m) • 280-275mya
Mesosaurus used its flattened tail and webbed feet to swim as
it sieved the shallows for shrimps and other tiny creatures.

DIMETRODON

die-met-roh-don "two kinds of teeth"
11 ft (3.5 m) • 280-250mya
Dimetrodon was a flesh eater, and the strange sail on its
back may have been for controlling its temperature.

The age of fishes

Some fishes developed into amphibians,
four-legged animals that laid their eggs in water.

BRANCHIOSAURUS

brank-ee-oh-saw-rus "gill lizard"
Up to 6 in (15 cm) • *280mya*
Young amphibians had external gills for
breathing in water, and Branchiosaurus
kept these after becoming an adult.

PLEUROCANTHUS

pleur-oh-canth-us "spiny sides"
Up to 30 in (75 cm) long • *350-*
265mya
Pleurocanthus was an early
shark, lived in freshwater lakes
and rivers, and had a long, eel-
like body.

DOLICHOSOMA

doh-lie-koh-so-ma "long body"
30 in (75 cm) • *340-270mya*
Dolichosoma lived in the water
hunting fishes and insects. It
looked like a snake, but was an
amphibian which had lost the
legs of its ancestors.

BOTHRIOLEPIS

both-ree-oh-lep-is "pitted scale"
Up to 12 in (30 cm) long • *370-345mya*
Bothriolepis grubbed in the mud for food
and may have been able to breathe air.

EOGYRINUS

ee-oh-guy-reen-us "early tadpole"
15 ft (4.6 m) • *340-270mya*
A huge amphibian with the head of a crocodile
and a long, eel-like body, Eogyrinus hunted
its prey through the swamps and lakes
of Europe.

DUNKLEOSTEUS

dunk-lee-ost-ee-us "Dunkle's bony creature"
Up to 30 ft (9m) long • *360-345mya*
Enormous Dunkleosteus ruled the seas and killed
its prey with its sharp, bony mouth plates.

First published in 2001 by
Miles Kelly Publishing Ltd
Bardfield Centre, Great Bardfield
Essex, U.K., CM7 4SL

This edition published by Barnes & Noble, Inc.

2 4 6 8 10 9 7 5 3 1

Author: Duncan Brewer

Project Manager: Ian Paulyn
Editors: Ruthie Boardman, Jenni Rainford
Editorial Director: Anne Marshall
Design: Debbie Meekcoms

Library of Congress Cataloging-in-Publication Data on file at the Library of Congress.

2002 Barnes & Noble Books

ISBN 0-7607-3753-3

Printed and bound in China

The abbreviation mya: million years ago